HERE NOR THERE

BY THE SAME AUTHOR

The Weakness
Gunpowder

HERE NOR THERE

Bernard O'Donoghue

Chatto & Windus
LONDON

Published by Chatto & Windus 1999

2 4 6 8 10 9 7 5 3 1

Copyright © Bernard O'Donoghue

First published in Great Britain in 1999 by
Chatto & Windus
Random House, 20 Vauxhall Bridge Road,
London SW1V 2SA

Random House Australia (Pty) Limited
20 Alfred Street, Milsons Point, Sydney,
New South Wales 2061, Australia

Random House New Zealand Limited
18 Poland Road, Glenfield,
Auckland 10, New Zealand

Random House South Africa (Pty) Limited
Endulini, 5A Jubilee Road, Parktown 2193, South Africa

Randon House UK Limited Reg. No. 954009

A CIP catalogue record for this book
is available from the British Library

ISBN 0 7011 6800 5

Papers used by Random House UK Limited are natural,
recyclable products made from wood grown in sustainable forests.
The manufacturing processes conform to the environmental
regulations of the country of origin.

Typeset by Deltatype Ltd, Birkenhead, Merseyside
Printed and bound in Great Britain by
The Guernsey Press Ltd,
Vale, Guernsey, Channel Islands.

For Ellen, Tom and Josie

'Something to do with territory makes them sing'
Norman MacCaig

Acknowledgements

Grateful acknowledgement is made to the following books, periodicals, newspapers and institutions where some of these poems first appeared: *Agenda, Atlanta Review, Clara News, Irish Times, Jellyfish Cupful* (eds B. Cokeliss and J. Fenton, Ulysses), *Tony Harrison, Loiner* (ed. Sandie Byrne, Oxford University Press), *Or volge l'anno* (ed. M. Sonsogni, Dedalus), *London Review of Books, Metre, New Poetry Chronicle, The New York Times, Oxford English, Oxford Magazine, Oxford Poetry, Poetry Ireland Review, Poetry* (Chicago), *Princeton University Chronicle, Religion and Literature, Seanchas Dúthalla, St John's College Notes* (Oxford), *Soundings, Stand, Stephen's Green, The Stinging Fly, Thumbscrew, The Times Literary Supplement, The Voice Box* (Royal Festival Hall), *Vintage New Writing 7, Voices, Wadham College Gazette, Zero.*

Contents

NECHTAN

When Bran and his more worldly-wise companions
Were settling happily in the idyll
Of the Island of Women, I spoilt it
For them – and for me – by being homesick
For Ireland. But then we found there was
No longer any welcome for us there.
Maybe out of resentment for the months
We'd spent living in Love's contentedness,
They wouldn't let us land, so now we're fated
To sail for ever in the middle seas, outcast
Alike from the one shore and the other.

THE OWLS AT WILLIE MAC'S

Having heard their cries across the fields,
I went outside into their element,
As blind in theirs as they in mine by day.
It was so dark, that late summer night,
I could see nothing of what caused
The ticking, and the steady tread
Of heavy boots towards me down the road
Until his bicycle was right alongside.
Still without seeing, I could smell the warmth
And kind breath of Nugget Plug and Guinness.
And then the voice, as from an invisible flame:

'When I worked at Willie Mac's, you'd hear them
Every night. You'd never see them, even when
They were right on top of you and sounding
Like a screech of brakes.' Who was he,
This dark-dressed, nearly extinct escaper
From the nineteen-fifties Saturday night?

There are some animals, the medievals said,
Whose eyes are so acute that they can, lidless,
Outstare the sun. He walked away from me,
Saving the battery by still not winding on
The squat flashlamp I pictured at the front.
Neither could my defective vision see
Him as he would be three months ahead,
Stretched in the road like the thirsty bittern
By a car that could hardly be expected
To pick him out against a wintering sky.

GHOULS

I see in the mirror that they've stolen
The skin from my mother's grave — flaky,
Blotched, dried out — and pulled it down
Over my face like an old stocking
For disguise. They've used more of it
To cover the backs of my hands;
I see it tauten between index-finger
And thumb as I wriggle into
An invisible glove. It is like
The obscene-looking puckers forming round
The thick nub of a deflating balloon.

The gel I soft-soap between the palms
And over my face cannot disguise the fact
That these are secondaries: signs of
Deeper-lying things the face can't hide.

COMMAND OF ENGLISH

in homage to Tony Harrrison

'the thin, smoky beauty of vain eloquence'

Kevin was always an hour late, or more.
He stammered so badly that the teacher
Gave up on him, and he didn't need
To learn anything. Johnny O'Connor
Was Down's Syndrome and cried when, every year,
He was kept back. He left junior school
At nineteen, still in high infants. When he
Pretended to recite, you couldn't tell
Whether or not what he was burbling was
'If all those endearing young charms.'

For all I know, I haven't seen him since.
He never took off his homemade cloth satchel
Or his coat, but he hypnotized us with
The pencil twiddled between his fingers:
So fast after fourteen years' practice
It was no more than an indistinct blur.
But Johnny had no luck to speak of.

T.W. in reverse, I would say 'luck'
For what the rest of them pronounced like 'look'.
And once at the bottom of an essay on
'What I would like to be when I grow up',
Was written 'Good command of English',
Which I didn't understand. Johnny sat late
Some nights, his ear six inches from
The HMV speaker, cronawning along
With Count John's rendition of 'Believe me',
His head on one side, balancing the dog's.

These days I'm better at interpreting,
Or so I fancy. In Johnny's remembered
Indecisive voice, I know every word
He meant: that *the heart that once truly loves*
Never forgets but as truly loves on
To the close, and further sentiments about
Gods and sunflowers and the setting sun.

THE DEFINITION OF LOVE

It's strange, considering how many lines
Have been written on it, that no-one's said
Where love most holds sway: neither at sex
Nor in wishing someone else's welfare,
But in spending the whole time over dinner
Apparently absorbed in conversation,
While really trying to make your hand take courage
To cross the invisible sword on the tablecloth
And touch a finger balanced on the linen.

A young curate of a parish in West Cork
Was told his mother was seriously ill
And he must come home to Boherbue
(In fact she was dead already; they had meant
To soften the blow). He drove recklessly
Through mid-Kerry and crashed to his death
In the beautiful valley of Glenflesk.
This was because he fantasized in vain
About touching her fingers one last time.

THE FAULTLINE

When there's a sprinkle of snow
In mid-January, yet not enough
To stop it turning vein-translucent.
When young relationships freeze
And snap. When death, suddenly,
Crops up in the conversation
And no-one quite remembers
Who raised the subject. As far past
Solstice as November was before it;
No sign of spring, and no
Going back. All just serving
To show, in case we'd forgotten,
Our faultline: that we're designed
To live neither together nor alone.

PIED PIPER

'Musheroons! Musheroons!', he shouted out,
Flipping the reins so that the foxy horse
Broke into a gallop for us, and the float
Lurched smoothly on its rubber wheels
Down the coarse meadow. Was it the same man
Who picked fights with the most peaceable
Family in the locality? – who
Hired a hackney car to drive to Mallow,
Twenty miles, to lodge a daft complaint
Against the postman? – who seized by the throat
The sole remaining helper on his farm,
A blind, willing old man of eighty,
Until he staggered for breath?

Maybe: because, although he had that first
Modern float, and brooded for years over designs
For a new house, he once left the threshing
So late in the year we could hear the grumble
Of the machine on Christmas Eve
As the damp sleet swept across his grain.
They had no children: him and his dapper wife
Who had the silkest stockings in the parish
And the highest heels, and who'd amassed
Twenty designer hats before she died.

The last time I saw him he was living
In an unfurnished mobile home. He spent
An hour and more patiently rolling
A polish-tin that limped on its opening-catch
Across the concrete floor, over and over,
To keep our anxious one-year-old from crying.
And I suddenly remembered his most foolish
Unexecuted enterprise of all:
That underneath his bed for twenty years
He stored the timber crates that held a *Simplex*
Milking machine for the stall he never built.

THE UVULAR *R*

i.m. Joan Hayes

The City on Sunday morning: turf briquettes
And Calor-gas rounded up in network compounds,
And the mist so dense you can hardly see
The ochres and light greens of Sunday's Well
Across the river. We were the Cork crowd;
We always lacked the definition
Of the more western voice and land in Kerry.
The south Cork coast, kind and all as it was,
Wasn't Dingle. Our gaeltacht was speckled,
Consonants that compromised and faded
On the mouth's roof like Communion wafers.
That our bruachs were riverbanks; that our local names
Took the English word for it: Newquarter,
Watergrasshill and Coalpits and Halfway.

PASSING LINDISFARNE

23 July 1997

We'd long passed the Bass Rock on our left,
Its gannets visible too fleetingly,
Now hardly more than low over the sea.
Since nothing soars, I turn back to the page
And form this mannered thought: that by this time
I've subscribed to you so long that I can place
Every reference to earlier issues
In the later sections.

Time can be made to last: put on our guard,
We can number every stone along the way
And every bone, close our eyes
And avoid once again each familiar pothole
That the bike's wheels learned to dodge around.

I must have been asleep: I'm picturing
The Old Court Castle at Kanturk
Whose mad, perfectionist designer wanted
A roof of coloured glass, a kind
That did not yet exist. I see it roofed,
Shining to the heavens. But now
We're pulling slowly into King's Cross,
All the divided tracks reconciling
And slowing to a stop.

THE DAUGHTER OF JAIRUS

for Pat-Joe Morley

There is an art to it that can't be learnt
By reading which roses to prune back
In their dormant season: you only know
From long experience which varieties
Flower on the old wood.

Our glass-cupboards you crafted perfectly
From wood saved when you dismantled
The organ-loft in the local church;
Our ceiling-boards were once the sprung floor
In the village dance-hall.

There's something else which tongues and grooves as well
Between the roses and the builder's pine:
The wood at the base of the furze-bush
Is dead, grey, dry – fit for nothing
But burning; yet on it grows

The vividest dark green and a gold
To put the newly risen sun to shame.
Everything fits: your apprentice-trade
Was coffin-making – six on a good day,
Flat out, with no meal-break.

The sawed pine first, shaped for the shoulders,
Narrowing by set proportion to the feet
(Set, according to some traditions,
One on the other). Then all lacquered,
Fitted out with fine handles of brass

To merit everlasting heaven's riches:
By this art to book your place, in the eyes
Of those who look up to the ceiling,
Among the ranks of the immortal dead.

PENCIL IT IN

Stumbling my fingers along the shelves,
I observe an interesting thing: books
I have had for more than thirty years
Feature my name in proud fountain-pen.
Now I'm reminded of it, I recall
Practising on rough paper to reach
Such a convincing dash of signature.

For a while they went slantwise,
In legible ballpoint; then anywhere,
With any implement: rollerpoint, red even.
Recently I am perturbed to find
I've started to sign in pencil. HB,
Naturally; but will the time come
When less permanent leads will do?
2B, 3B, 4B. . . . .

A FOOL AT DOON BRIDGE

'Et ai be faih co.l fols en pon'
Bernart de Ventadorn *c.* 1170

He couldn't wait for the swallows to come back,
So they sent him down to the Araglen Bridge
Where he'd last seen them, cutting low
Through the arches. 'The summer's nearly here,'
They said, 'So keep a close eye on the river.
As soon as you see it starting to slow down,
Get back quick and tell us, and we'll fill
Baths and buckets and kettles and warming-pans.'

He hung over the centre arch all day,
Watching the water carving its way down
Towards him. He saw the collies flickering
Invisibly in the mud, as good as mud
Themselves. Occasionally the level seemed
To drop, but when you closed one eye (like this)
And raised a finger, the brown hole in the bank
You measured it against didn't make a stir.

This was the place as well where he had seen
A dipper in the March flood working the silt
Beneath the rags of plastic in the blackthorn.
He'd just begun to remind himself of that
For comfort, when suddenly he spotted
The mocker in the branches overhead,
Tail bent downwards like a snapped twig. 'Look, Dan!'
He called to himself out loud, 'The cuckoo!'

LONG WORDS

I can't remember what enterprise it was
We were breaking to each other
That made Denis John give me the word:
'My grandmother' (I knew her: a woman
Forever at her prayers) 'says
The longest word in the world is
Transcranscriptiation.'

So far I haven't found one longer than it,
For all my browsing in the Dictionary.
'Though I didn't go to school myself',
The old people were fond of saying,
'Still I met the scholars coming home.'

NOT BELIEVING IN CROCODILES

for a child-sceptic

'And there be also in that country many camels: that is a
little beast like a goat, that is wild, and he liveth by the air
and eateth nought, ne drinketh nought, at no time. And he
changeth his colour often-time, now in one colour and
now in another colour; and he may change him into all
manner colours that he wanteth, save only into red and
white.'

Mandeville's Travels, c. 1360

Still, why should you credit this unlikely beast,
Eyes silent, frozen-smiled, with a stopped clock
Ticking in its stomach, when you think of
The unsubstantiated tales that have been tried
On you: horses that could talk; fairies
Who traded in teeth left under pillows;
Genial old men in red and white fur coats
With sacks of toys; people with heads beneath
Their shoulders or with leafy feet as sun-shades.

And yet you'd seen these leathern comics
Often enough: you'd hung on the rails waiting
For their slow and threatening wink,
A sly concession that they're only
Pretending to be there: as real as Hook
Or Peter's powder that empowered flight.

But how did you learn to distrust appearance?
You'd never been in Dan Riordan's forge,
Watching the bellows drive the sparks to make
The horseshoes whiten like sucked ice-lollies
Almost to non-existence, before re-emerging
Surly and blue-black in the water.
There all the time. Tell me which you saw first,
Josie, the anvil or the rhino's head,
So as to know which to compare with which.

THE MARK OF CAIN

They misinterpreted My purposes
In imposing it. I'm not concerned
With Cain, with whether he's killed or not;
I wanted to demonstrate that people,
Without any written instruction,
Will look away: not mock; instinctively
Not maim those afflicted enough already.

But Cain did die. And woe to the hand
By which he died! Woe too to the day
When Cain woke to find the port-wine stain
Had vanished from his temple. For that's the day
They'll fall on him and rend him limb from limb.

HERMES

'And now I long to be a poet
With something good to say.'

i.m. Denis O'Connor, 1917–1997

Just as I'm happier walking in the dark
Of night and feel more safe in planes
Than on the ground, I'm less at ease
Among the living than the dead.
For years I've specialized in writing
Letters to the bereaved, a brief
From a licensed afterlife, consoling
Children, widowers and widows.

But who am I to write to about you,
Denis, who made your own way? I'd like
To honour your unrivalled singing,
Your melojeon, and your wit-barbs;
Your merriment among the dancers,
And your vamped mouth-organ. Who do I remind
How you could run up the twenty rungs
Of a ladder standing in the middle
Of the yard, our stilted boy?

You had the excitement of the hare,
And a like form, away from the everyday.
You had the fox's glamour, the perfectly
Made out-of-the-ordinariness
Of that thrush's nest, sealed with spit,
You showed us above the arum lilies.
We admired, but didn't understand
That you were Hermes, bearing messages
From the past, and must return, like summer
Out over the top of the fairy-thimbles.

Who dug your grave, Denis,
Since you dug everyone's?
Who carried your coffin?
There's no-one in the parish
Who would not push to the front
Of the crowd to bear you.
Are we now at liberty to call you
Dansel, the venerated, unaccounted-for
Nickname of your family,
That no-one spoke in your presence –
Out of some sentiment: tact? or fear?
Love maybe. In the silence
After your death, may we speak it now?

In the grave, shall all be renewed?
Your celebrity? Will this letter do?
No: by way of postscript I remind us all
Of a late-December night when you were old
And sick and looking for a drive
To help you get your messages up home.
It wasn't easy to make out what
You were mumbling, with the drink.
'Christmas is the worst time of all
For the person living on their own.'

CHRISTMAS

Despite the forecast's promise,
It didn't snow that night;
But in the morning, flakes began
To glide all right.
Not enough to cover roads
Or even hide the grass;
But enough to change the light.

THE ROAD TO DOON SCHOOL

for Den Joe Murphy

Buachaill dána dob ea Seán Ó Riain.
Bhí dúil mór aige in úlla.
How could a journey of just over a mile
Take us an hour and a quarter, as we pushed,
Shouted and peered over two *glaises*,
Past the furzy glen, up the ceannadas
Or down past Ring's Fort, asking Julia
The time, picking lady's smock or prising out
Cold shamrock with two upright fingernails?

We planned the orchard-raids more often
Than we executed them, a theme of heroes
– *The grim Dutch gunners eyed them well –*
Of threatened capture and strategic flight
Down Glounthane hill. Mrs Galvin's eaters
Or the huge green cookers we could see
Through the blackthorn hedges where we aimed
Grey County Council chippings in an arc
To crash on the roof of Buckley's outhouse.

Once in the shock of silence that followed,
We realized, too late for getaway,
That Jerry Buckley was bearing down on us.
Without a look or headshake of rebuke,
He dispensed to us robbers a gwáil
Of the sweetest fruit his orchard had to offer.

'DOGS, WOULD YOU LIVE FOR EVER?'

Frederick the Great

She's bent at stool, as the saying is,
Next to her deathbed. Her arched back
Is like white fish
That has been too long in the fridge,
Greyed at the spine-bones.

Crying, she says 'this is the worst now.'
I say 'of course it's not.
You did as much for children
Often enough.'

But of course it was: the scene
Comes back, untriggered, more
Rather than less often,
Oddly enough.

I'd prefer you to wait outside.

TIMMY BUCKLEY OBSERVES THE PLEIADES

It's January on a moonless, frosty night;
But they're not visible here, the ice-cluster
Sisters. They're hiding in North Cork
In '53, observed by Timmy Buckley
Who's waiting for the end of night milking
To fill his paper-stoppered whiskey bottle.

'The Seven Sisters, called the Pleiades,
Were the daughters of a famous king of Greece
Whose lands overflowed with milk and honey.
Electra was the fairest one of them.
There was this rich man in Kerry long ago
Who had a prize bull called Currens Atlas . . .'

Timmy had a name as a bit of a poet,
So we'd leave him to it. And once that's said,
Suddenly I see them here, low in the Bull
And realize they stood there all the time,
Waiting. I fix on them, knowing you're out as well
Watching, on whatever eminence.

Do you think that the eye's determined drawstring
That leads from me to them homes back to you,
As reliably as the mind's to Timmy Buckley? –
That such weightless communication
Influences the far receiving heart
To shrink the gap in space as well as time?

FROM *PIERS PLOWMAN*, c. 1375

I

While I was dreaming, Nature enlightened me,
Calling my name and saying to take notice
While she led me on through all the world's marvels.
And on this great mountain named Earth, I imagined,
I was first led away to find out in practice
How God might be loved through observing his creatures.
The sun I saw, and the sea, and the sand by the shore;
I saw how the birds make their nests in the trees;
No man has the skill to equal the least of them.
Who on earth, then I wondered, tutored the magpie
To arrange all the sticks that she lays on to breed?
No joiner, I'm certain, could make a dome like it.
What kind of a builder might follow that blueprint?
There were visions besides that I marvelled at further:
Other bird pairs that sheltered their eggs
In the deepest seclusion on moor and in marsh, in swamp
           or on water,
So no-one could find them but the two of themselves.

Then I looked out to sea and beyond to the stars.
Such marvels I saw I can hardly describe them:
Flowers in the wood of beautiful colours,
And all shining through the green grass and brown earth.
Some were rank and some scented: a magical world
That I haven't the time or the skill to describe.
There's provision enough here, faith has no doubt,
For no life ever given lacked the means of survival,
An element to live in and a reason for living.
First the wild worm lives in wet earth;
The fish lives in water, the cricket in fire.
The curlew by nature lives on the air,

23

So of any bird   its meat is the cleanest.
Animals live   on grass, grain and rootcrops:
This shows that man too   has a natural food
Which is not only bread   but sustained faith and love.

(B–text xi, xii)

2

The Trinity is like   a torch or a candle –
Which are wax and a wick   entwining together
And a fire flaming   out of the two of them.
Just as wax and wick   and the heat work together
To foster a flame   and a beautiful glow
Which are useful to workers   to see by at night,
So do the Father, the Son and the Spirit
Conjoin to produce in us   love and belief
Which melt their sins   out of every person.
And just as sometimes you see,   watching a torch,
That the flame will blow out   though the wick is still
                                                    glowing
And there's no gleam of light,   so low the wick smoulders,
Likewise the Spirit's grace   elicits no mercy
From those strange creatures   that want to destroy
Faithful love   or the life that God made.

And as coal merely glowing   gives no cheer to workers
That toil and keep watch through the night in the winter,
In the way that a blaze does   from twigs or a candle,
No more will the Trinity   acting together
Provide any grace   or forgiveness from sin
Till the Holy Ghost blazes   and bursts into flame.
But the Spirit will glow   no more than an ember
Until faithful love   bends over it, blowing;
Then he burns like fire   on the Father and Son
And melds both into mercy   – as you see in the winter

24

Icicles on house-eaves   through the heat of the sun
Melt in a minute   to mist and to water.

(B—text xvii)

3

'*Consummatum est*', said Christ,   and began to pass out,
Pale as a prisoner   that's dying the death.
The lord of life and light   laid his eyelids together.
The day fled in fear   and the sun turned black;
Walls trembled and split,   the whole world quavered.

(B—text xviii, 57–61)

GETTING OUT

for John Fuller, 1–1–1997

> 'The opposite of love is not hate but fear'
> Herbert MacCabe

These days what fills me with the greatest
Sense of achievement is getting out
Of doing things. So, by way of holiday,
I've taken to pretending that I'm not
Native to this town but only passing through.
I buy, say, a cappuccino and a roll,
And lean against a tree in my own garden,
Taking the air and watching the locals:
Such pilgrims, for example, as the coot
Who, for all her reputation for being daft,
Knows what she's doing as she steps down
Along the bank to enfold her reflection
And swim away, the two of them. Overhead
I might see the silver underbelly
Of a flight of pigeons. Or I could visit
The shopping quarter to experience
Something I've often noticed: the strange echo
Of the mountain falcon's mew in Tesco's checkout.

SILVERFISH

A category error, philosophically speaking,
Or a flaw in genetic coding that makes
These blurs of clockwork mercury
Wheel along the dry floor without wheels,
Like monks out of their cloisters
Or the no-pace-perceived tree-creeper
That scurries up the branches like a mouse.

FEMMER

for Eugene O'Connell

Despite its soft ephemerality,
They say the growth of elder is a sign
Of age-long human habitation.
Under the elders in our decaying farmyard
Stands the last sugán chair, rotted at all
Its skilfully carved joints, so the lightest
Tenant would cause it to collapse.

There's one like it in the dying house
Of Padraig O'Keeffe at Glounthane Cross:
Not our Glounthane, but the one near Cordal
Where my forebears came from. I stole from there
A small piece of lino, geography-shaped
Like the booty-map in *Treasure Island*,
Where it lay among foxed holy pictures.

The stairs are dangerous; and no matter
How hard you strain you can't fool yourself
Into hearing his spectrally played polkas there,
Even in that valley of ghost-houses.
You have more chance five miles east the road,
Up through the forestry where the Blackwater
Rises and you can imagine anything
In that wind that blows at you all the way
From the Atlantic which, astonishingly,
You can see: its last gleam of silver
Both at Tralee and off the Blasket islands.

PRESERVATIVE

Even though ice melts quickly
Before the sun's direct rays
So you can't see where it has been,
Yet there are places of shade
And protection – in rushes
Or in hedges – where it stays
Almost to midday. You too
In your grey dress are fading,
Except in moments of shadow
Where your face is found in full,
Perhaps because your last cheek-kiss
Was cold as currency.

HURLING COUNTIES

'Ireland is Connacht'
Yeats

This barbarian's sport, you'd expect it

Well to the west, in Hell or Connacht.
But it's not a wetlands game; it's played
On the shaved lawns near the few surviving

Avenues of chestnuts in the Pale,
In Waterford, Kilkenny and East Cork,
Near the harbours where the ferries sail from.

You can see the respectable goalposts
Through the porthole, saluting the foghorn.

Meanwhile in the west the stuck pig's bladder
Is all you need to start a soccer match.
So who were in the gaelic teams? The law-

abiders and successes; those who minded
Their books and qualified for the Guards,
The Civil Service, or for teaching.

Amhrán:
Subs would be clerics, or fellows attached to
such rich institutions as had the resources
to stretch to the cost of a bagful of hurleys,
a sliothar of pigskin and a carload of jerseys
from a sports-shop like Clery's.

CANKER

Think of those mornings when you got away
With the sore throat, listening in warmth
To doors slam and cars start and people
Dashing down steps with bags and boxes.
By nine quiet had descended; by ten
Depression and a long prophetic sense
Of empty space and time. Half-dozing:

Thermometers; dreamt starched white skirts,
Too late attractive; grapes; making the best,
Until by early afternoon the rain
Sets in and the back-pains make it hard
To sustain the subterfuge any longer.
Bear with me while I change into

A more comfortable position.
– This is fun, isn't it? What kind of mind
Homes in on such reflections on a day
Of breeze and rose, in the sweet air up here
That rejoices in the sun? (What was his nickname –
That old cranky, plain-speaking Yorkshire barman

At St Jude's who fixed you with his dentured grin:
'In two months I'll be pushing up daisies'?
What a bore he was! None of the young fresh folks
(And small blame to them) could bear to be
Left alone with him. 'Canker' possibly?
Or if it wasn't it should have been.)

REAPER-AND-BINDER

Voices were lost as the reaper-and-binder
Went clacketing past, spitting out at you showers
Of gold you embraced with your arms overfull,
So the sheaves slithered down from the grip of their
                                                  bindings
As children, incompetent, slide out of jumpers.

At night on your pillow your ears went on singing
In time to its music by echo and echo
While your awn-scalded forearms still throbbed from its
                                                  fallout.

THE DROWNED BLACKBIRD

from the Irish of Séamus Dall Mac Cuarta, c. 1700

Pretty daughter of Con O'Neill,
  Asleep at last from mourning your bird,
Don't let your people listening in
  Know that your rest has been disturbed.

Of course you want to hear it sing
  As it sang just now on your window-sill.
But heartache is only a sign of love,
  So don't wring your hands. Come on! Be still!

Such wringing of hands! Give them a rest,
  My little gull, and wipe your eye.
Pretty daughter of Con O'Neill,
  For the blackbird's flight why should we cry?

Song

My gull that grew from the king of Ulster's kings,
Stay as you are! Surely it's more to your liking
To play back the blackbird's song on the branch's edge
Than to dwell all day long on the lime round his lightening
                                   bones.

UNKNOWNST TO THE PEOPLE

The small boy's clothes smelt terrible:
Goats, maybe pig droppings – or something worse.
We had to defumigate the car
After we'd unwisely picked him up
Out of the rain on his way to shop
In Carraiganima (where Art O'Leary
Met his poetic martyrdom).

A strange accent: north of England
Overlaid with the aspirates of North Cork.
He told us about his Mum and Dads,
And how they'd built the palisade themselves
From bits and pieces of discarded wood.

All that summer, though we never saw
The occupants, we watched the holding grow
In confidence on its small quarter-acre:
The washing hung to dry; plastic buckets
Lying round. And always the blue of woodsmoke.

When we came back next spring, the whole place
Was gone, only marked by soaking, charred wood.
A year later again, and green grass was growing
To the neatly locked gate at the roadside.
We asked around, but no-one seemed to know
Where they had gone to, or why,
And everyone looked downward to the ground.

THE PLEASURES OF THE CIRCUS

for Marius Kwint

Pleasant are the clowns who wet the people
Sitting in front, and drive children's cars,
Parping their horns.
Pleasant the trapese-artists
Who swing by the canvas, high
Over the ground.
Pleasant the tigers that steal round the ring
And squat with resentment
On starry stools.
Pleasant the ice-cream in its melting tub
That you eat in the interval
With a cracked wood paddle.
Pleasant the band whose can-can blares
Across to the mountains
From the town park.

> Acrobats are the highest;
> Elephants the biggest;
> Lions the sulkiest;
> Trombones the brayingest;
> Ice-cream's the coldest;
> Clowns the funniest;
> Zora the loveliest;
> Horses the fastest;
> Seats the hardest;
> Car-parks the muddiest;
> Parents the rattiest.

SATURDAY EVENING

after Leopardi

You'd hear the mower late into the evening,
Anxious to get the whole meadow down
To ripen in the sabbath sun. The blacksmith's bike
Passing down home at twenty-five to ten,
The smith singing out the prospect
Of the full day off. Cleaning Sunday shoes,
Listening to Céili House, interspersed
With the thrush through the open window.

Look: *'red sky at night, shepherd's delight'*.

But that was the best of it. You were woken
At six a.m. by the insistent rain,
Falling on the hay, and making it muddy
Underfoot. To put a good face on it,
Your mind tilts towards the next week's vigil.

'ROPED FOR THE FAIR'

Ivor Gurney

Originally there was nothing strange
About him, except that he was quiet
And often listened to the BBC.
A good farmer, his hay was always in
By mid-August, nor did he ever need
To work on Sunday. Even in the fifties
He was able to buy modern machines
By some miracle of husbandry.

The odd thing about it was, of course,
That it was the new sixties affluence
Which turned him revolutionary,
Until one April day he studiously
Placed his Taiwanese transistor underneath
His tractor wheels and drove over it,
Back and forth, twenty times, until he could
No longer see its cunning inner workings.

He had, to put it plainly, lost his reason.
He read books about Russia, and talked
(When he talked at all) about Mao Tse Tung.
The family turned a blind eye to it
And made excuses for him at Mass where he
No longer went. On Sunday morning
He'd walk out and look south-west to Mangerton
Smiling, leaning over his five-barred gate.

He'd even, in a further stage of mania,
Started to feel sorry for his body,
Its hardworking limbs and members: and how
It couldn't even sleep without invasion
From Consciousness who crept around the door
In the half-light and was waiting silent,
Menacing, at the bed-end when he woke up,
Ready to resume its joyless, daily vigil.

It seemed as though he'd – too late – fallen in love
With something he'd once been, and then been
Deprived of. He cast around for images
To fix what was slipping: the big Pyrex plate
Of thawing ice that no longer quite touched
The side of the barrel so a sole finger
Could push it under the surface of the water;
His life seemed, like that, unwieldy.

Or like bread that has been kneaded out
Until it's too floppy for any baker's hands.
Or maybe like a plane caught suddenly
In pockets of turbulence which cause
Its wings to rock and quiver in a wild
And flimsy reaching out for stableness.
It couldn't last, and in the course of things
Inevitably, they carted him away,

Kindly enough. After nine months of treatment
He came back: 'a new man', they said.
He spoke, if that was possible, even less
Than before. He rode a bike to Mass (something
No-one did in those days) so he needn't
Make conversation by falling in step
With neighbours or by sitting in with them.
He still leant across his gate, except

Now he wasn't smiling at the prospect
Of the mountains. Neither was he probing
For an image to enclose it, once for all.
He looked in vain for happy living things
That might bring him back to some affection:
But the straightbacked greenfinch on the berries
Scorned him in the grudging drawing out
Of the misted early days of February;

The blinding crimson of its brother goldfinch
Inclined him towards panic. Could he hold out
Until the warblers came again in April?
Were the birds now saying *'Change for a pound.*
Change for a pound'? Not that he was without
All hope or ambition: biding his time,
He was waiting for the chance to go along
With the first decent flood of the coming spring.

DACRYOMA

i.m. Catherine Beeston

Although we recognize
that it's a medical condition,
this inability to cry,
there are other things
to be considered: refusal
to mourn, or to make our friends
mourn; the will to go on.

Strange as the word seems
on first hearing, there are stranger:
'bravery', 'courage', 'grace', say.
And there are more strange
conditions too: like walking onwards
with your books, hardly raising
your head, more inclined to smile.

REMNANTS

For years we never took there anything
That would do in a real house: just a fridge
That leaked its gas, a toaster you had to
Hold down by hand, a rocking-chair thrown out
From an old people's home in North Yorkshire.
The carpet was an offcut with a hole in it
Covered by the table. The record-player
Worked fitfully, slowing year by year.

Since then, things are both worse and better:
A new fridge, bought cut-price in Barrack Street;
On the other hand, a typewriter
That looks perfect, but doesn't work at all.

And suddenly, I see what it was all about:
That begging for bed-irons, spotted near gateposts
In Dingle and given with grave perplexity:
'Tá meirg orthu'; why I'd rather pay
For these dying objects than replacements.
I hoped thereby to bring back to life the people:
Jack Sweeney, Phil Micheál and Mary-Ann John Riordan
Who prayed and prayed well into her nineties.

(Tá meirg orthu: they are rusty)

KILLARNEY

'It could only happen in Ireland'
                    Flann O'Brien

While we were waiting for the bird-watcher group,
We idly fixed our binoculars upon
An American grand party in the grounds
By the fringes of the lake (where we could see
Also, we thought, turnstones). A barbecue,
With wine glasses, brown arms, red dresses
In the sun: people casually and idly
Drinking and eying each other over,
Dreaming of the likely hotel afternoon.
Meanwhile the heron lifted herself away,
In no great hurry, over the water
To the grey middle island where the saint's
Oratory was, or so the locals told you.
Ready for any eventuality,
We tucked our trousers inside our woollen socks.

REASSURANCE

And from his death-bed, suddenly he said
At the end of a life of faith: 'Peggy,
I hope things are as we always thought they were,'
And she assured him that Heaven certainly awaited.

Personally, I hope not. Because, if Hell and Heaven
Are assorted by the just God we learnt of,
We can have little prospect of salvation:
We who have turned to the sports news,
Leaving the hanged girl from Srebenica
On the front page, just as before we watched
Without a protest while the skeleton-soldier
Burned by the steering-wheel on the road to Basra;
We too who are so sure about the frailties
Of those who failed to do anything about
The Famine, or who'd turn up the volume
To drown the clanking of the cattle-trucks
That pulled away eastward in black and white.

REDWINGS

What were they playing at, those strange thrushes
That crowded the ground with hardly more
Than a *peep!*, disguised as the greatest
Songsters of the spring? Maybe they were hatching
A plan to fool the first-winter calves
Who can't make out what's happened to the sun
Or why their grass has been reduced
To cold clumps of marram. They never died,
It seemed, but flew off in low sweeps
Over the neighbouring ditches, onward to
The cold foothills of the mountains,
Of Caherbarnagh and the Paps. 'Farewell,
Fieldfare!', we said to them and to their kind,
Not sure if it was a dream, their winter break.

CHILD LANGUAGE ACQUISITION

The first skill you learned in our townland
Was how to sustain a double conversation
With a couple not on speaking terms.
'Was she wearing a mauvish scarf?' 'I think
She' 'Tell your father the horse is being used
For the creamery.' 'All right. He knows, I think.
There might have been a bit of red in it.'
'She borrowed it from her sister so. The one
She wears for Mass is brown'. 'Before eleven
At the earliest.' 'And she never smiled again.'

More crucially, you had to learn which families
Were feuding, so as not to stray
Into damaging allusion to the enemy.
John Tim had never spoken to the Sheas
Since they cut off the corner of a field
In nineteen-thirty-four. One crisis came
When his brother saw you talking
To their sister, after he'd given you
Half a crown for your Confirmation.
The moral question: had you to give it back?

So there was nothing new for us about
The dialogical imagination.
All useful training for the life
Of letters, learning to distinguish
Between revisionists in the horse and trap,
Modernists off to the pictures, realists
Drinking tea from a gallon in the meadow,
And historicists taking it all in.

MARRIAGE MADE IN HEAVEN

Furtively the new stems
Of clematis grip hands
Behind the apple-tree's back.
You can't make them if
They haven't a mind to.
Try it: lift one slender arm
And twine it, however gently,
Round the other. As soon as
You've turned away, it will
Let go and hang its head,
Considering who to ask next,
Now that the spell's been broken.

FALLOUT

for Peter and Ursula Dronke

In a certain town (better not say its name)
It rained for a whole day, and as a consequence
All the people went mad except for one
Who'd been lying at home in a whiskey stupor.
When the rain stopped, he tottered out
Amazed at what he saw. Everyone
Was crazy. A lawyer wore a nappy
And a bib; a teacher strutted round naked;
A doctor was spitting high above him,
Exulting when he reached a window-sill.
One man, deep in thought, ripped his clothes from chin
To ankles; one was hitting nothing; one was
Shouldering the air, grunting with the effort.
One tried to make out he was the king.

They see the newcomer, yawning
And scratching his poll in puzzlement,
And they don't much like his attitude.
Thinking it's him that's off his head,
They corner him. They slap his face
And pull his neck and yank his ears,
Finally drawing blood. He apologizes
And tries to run. But they are on to him
At once, shouting and cursing. Several times
He falls under their blows and gets up again
Until finally he limps home, mud-covered
And with blacked eyes. He forces the door shut
Behind him, listening in terror as his friends
Beg for his body from the street outside.

(from the Provençal of Peire Cardenal)

47

CLARA

To climb the mountain it's necessary to cross
From the reservoir behind Mountleader
Through a walled corner which appears to be
Both house and trees. You have to negotiate
A small window into a kitchen-copse
Where a sycamore is growing through
A hearthstone. Nobody seems to know
Who lived there, not even the old people
Whose grandmothers remembered when there were
Nine houses in the half-acre of elders
Behind the Old Screen. In the autumn,
If you stand very still and listen,
You can hear, you fancy, behind the rustling
Of the leaves in the endless westerly,
Women's voices, quietly about their business.

THE DRUMMERS

i.m. Angus Macintyre on 31 March 1995

The first twelve days of April are old March,
So from here we proceed with caution
For a while. Yet the fritillaries
Have already hung magic lanterns
From their green javelins, so it must be safe
For the roses to shoot again: those roses
That Angus mocked yearly because they put out
Elaborate mauve feelers before the last frost
And paid the penalty, like over-eager students
Rushing to judgment too enthusiastically.

The chiffchaff's back, early this year,
And the woodpeckers are drumming away.
For some odd reason, this morning
Those drummers, who normally startle
At the first sign of observation
And flee in disappointing lifts and swoops
Into the distance, hold their stations,
Beating a tattoo as if their lives
Depended on it. When my arms and neck ache
And I move on, they move ahead as well
And drum again before me, like scouts
With some message too urgent to ignore.

KILMACOW

A chapel in a graveyard in a fort,
And Denis Hickey, sitting by the gate
With his knuckle-headed blackthorn,
A benevolent Dis who's wondering out loud
'Where can I take ye now?'

We'd started in a place not that easy
To find: 'The Hole at the Corner',
A bend in the river where yellow flag-iris
Climbed from the bank to the claimed field
Where another fort had been filled in.

And in between he'd taken us to see
A famine-graveyard, marked only
By an iron cross that was ignorant
Of its own meaning and leaked rust
Into the nettles like the good knight's armour.

We'll stay here for a while, to absorb
These rings of meaning: the outer town
Holding its dead to its heart, which has also held
Kneeling parishioners with caps under one knee
And the fixed foot ever the higher.

We'll stay because it's clear, in all the silence,
That descent back to Avernus isn't so easy.

WESTERING HOME

Though you'd be pressed to say exactly where
It first sets in, driving west through Wales
Things start to feel like Ireland. It can't be
The chapels with their clear grey windows,
Or the buzzards menacing the scooped valleys.
In April, have the blurred blackthorn hedges
Something to do with it? Or possibly
The motorway, which seems to lose its nerve
Mile by mile. The houses, up to a point,
With their masoned gables, each upper window
A raised eyebrow. More, though, than all of this,
It's the architecture of the spirit;
The old thin ache you thought that you'd forgotten –
More smoke, admittedly, than flame;
Less tears than rain. And the whole business
Neither here nor there, and therefore home.

TER CONATUS

Sister and brother, nearly sixty years
They'd farmed together, never touching once.
Of late she had been coping with a pain
In her back, realization dawning slowly
That it grew differently from the warm ache
That resulted periodically
From heaving churns on to the milking-stand.

She wondered about the doctor. When,
Finally, she went, it was too late,
Even for chemotherapy. And still
She wouldn't have got round to telling him,
Except that one night, watching television,
It got so bad she gasped, and struggled up,
Holding her waist. 'D'you want a hand?', he asked,

Taking a step towards her. 'I can manage',
She answered, feeling for the stairs.
Three times, like that, he tried to reach her.
But, being so little practised in such gestures,
Three times the hand fell back, and took its place,
Unmoving at his side. After the burial,
He let things take their course. The neighbours watched

In pity the rolled-up bales, standing
Silent in the fields, with the aftergrass
Growing into them, and wondered what he could
Be thinking of: which was that evening when,
Almost breaking with a lifetime of
Taking real things for shadows,
He might have embraced her with a brother's arms.